The Hymn

Vocal Solos for Medium Voice by Nancy Walters

TABLE OF CONTENTS

FOREWORD

Music plays an important role in the life of the church. That's why, as a church soloist, I've always wanted the music I sing to be edifying to those who listen, and to reflect Who God is and my love for Him. I've discovered that finding "good" solo music that does all this is not always easy. Several years ago this concern led me to my hymnbook. While reading through some of my favorite hymns, I was struck anew by the depth and beauty of their words. These were the words I wanted to sing -- only in a more contemporary style. So, one by one, I gave each hymn a fresh and different setting which I hoped would enhance their meaning. The result is THE HYMN SOLOIST.

Here is a collection of nine completely new settings of old and familiar hymn texts. They're appropriate for both formal or informal settings, morning and evening worship, Communion services, and there's even one for the Advent Season.

It's a joy for me to share these solos with you. As you sing them, I hope the words will take on a new and deeper meaning for you personally, and will be a blessing to those who listen.

Thanks, Mom and Dad, for teaching me to love the old hymns, and, more importantly, to believe in the One about Whom they were written. This book is dedicated to you.

Nancy Walters
Houghton, New York
June, 1991

JUST AS I AM

Words by Charlotte Elliott

Music by Nancy Walters

wilt re-ceive, will wel-come me, par-don me, cleanse and re-lieve; Be-

cause Thy prom-ise I be-lieve,___ O__ Lamb of God,__ I

come,___ I come.___ I come to You just as I am.

I come to You just as I__ am.

HOLY, HOLY, HOLY

Words by Reginald Heber

Music by Nancy Walters

17 *a tempo*

Ho - ly, ho - ly, ho - ly, mer - ci - ful and might - y!

a tempo

21

God in Three per - sons, *poco rit.* bless - ed Trin - i - ty! *a tempo*

poco rit.

a tempo

25 *rit.* **A little faster** (♩ = 88) *mf*

2. Ho - ly, ho - ly,

ten.

rit. *ten.* *mf*

29

ho - ly, all the saints a - dore Thee, Cast - ing down their

side Thee per - fect in pow'r and love _____ and in pur - i-

ty.

Ho - ly, ho - ly, ho - ly, Lord __ God __ Al - might - y,

All Thy works shall praise, all Thy works shall praise Thy name in earth and sky and

FAIREST LORD JESUS

Words from *Münster Gesängbuch*

Music by Nancy Walters

16

bloom - ing spring; Je - sus is fair - er, Je - sus is

pur - er, He makes our sor-row-ing spir - it sing.

3. Fair is the sun - shine, fair is the moon-light, And bright ___ the

I SURRENDER ALL

Words by Judson W. Van de Venter

Music by Nancy Walters

COME, THOU LONG–EXPECTED JESUS

Words by Charles Wesley

Music by Nancy Walters

25

born a child, and yet a King. Born ___ to reign in us for-

ev - er, ___ now Thy gra-cious King-dom bring,

now Thy gra-cious King-dom bring.

3. By Thy own e-ter-nal Spir - it rule in all our hearts a-

I WILL SING OF MY REDEEMER

Words by Philip P. Bliss

Music by Nancy Walters

Sing,— O sing _____ of my Re-deem-er,— with His

blood _____ He pur-chased me; On— the cross _____ He sealed my

par-don, _____ paid the debt and made me free.

2. I will

blood _____ He pur-chased me; _____ On _ the cross _____ He sealed my

par-don,_ paid the debt _____ and made me free. On _ the

cross _____ He sealed my par-don,_ paid the debt, and He

made me free.

8ba

SATISFIED

Words by Clara T. Williams

Music by Nancy Walters

ALL THE WAY MY SAVIOR LEADS ME

Words by Fanny J. Crosby

Music by Nancy Walters

NEARER, STILL NEARER

Words by Lelia N. Morris

Music by Nancy Walters

pride, give me but Je-sus my Lord cru-ci -fied.

4. Near - er, still near - er, while life shall last, 'til safe in

glo - ry my an - chor is cast; Thru end - less